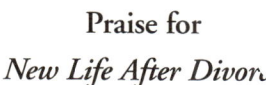

Praise for
New Life After Divorce

"When divorce drains you of hope, this book can refill you with encouragement, optimism, and plans for a brighter future. My friend Bill Butterworth isn't an armchair pontificator; his wise and biblical advice flows out of his own heart-break and new life. Let your journey toward recovery begin now!"

> —LEE STROBEL, author of *The Case for Christ*
> and *The Case for a Creator*

"If you're divorced, then you're in the club—The Walking Wounded Club—where a lifetime membership came wrapped in a broken heart. Come to these words and hear about the only One who is able to carry the wounded—our merciful God, who heals and restores and redeems. He is the God of Glory, and He promises to make your broken life new."

> —ANGELA THOMAS, speaker and author of
> *Do You Think I'm Beautiful?*

"Bill Butterworth's *New Life After Divorce* is a channel of God's love to people in pain. Divorce breaks God's heart and the hearts of its victims, but Bill reminds us through his own vulnerability that it happens—even in the church. By reading *New Life After Divorce,* you'll be assured that hope can live again, even when you think it can't."

> —THOM LEMMONS, author of *Jabez*

"Bill takes you through an honest journey of life after divorce, providing you with encouragement, hope, and practical suggestions for personal growth and healing."

> —DR. ROGER TIRABASSI, pastoral counselor

"*New Life After Divorce* is a light for an often dark path. Bill Butterworth's honesty, humor, and vision for the future provide practical direction as well as graceful encouragement for those going through the difficulties of divorce. Thank you, Bill, for this much-needed handbook of hope!"

—SHARON HERSH, author of *"Mom, Everyone Else Does!"*
and *"Mom, I Hate My Life!"*

"Many know Bill Butterworth as a master communicator and humorist. In *New Life After Divorce* you will come to know him as a friend who walks humbly, authentically, and candidly with those who know firsthand the ugly reality of marriage breakdown and who wonder if there is any hope for their future. Bill has lived each word of this book. You will find life in every page."

—GENE APPEL, associate pastor, Willow Creek
Community Church

New Life
after divorce

workbook

New Life
after divorce

workbook

the promise of hope beyond the pain

Bill Butterworth

WATERBROOK
PRESS

NEW LIFE AFTER DIVORCE WORKBOOK
PUBLISHED BY WATERBROOK PRESS
2375 Telstar Drive, Suite 160
Colorado Springs, Colorado 80920
A division of Random House, Inc.

All Scripture quotations, unless otherwise indicated, are taken from the *New American Standard Bible®.* © Copyright The Lockman Foundation 1960, 1962, 1963, 1968, 1971, 1972, 1973, 1975, 1977, 1995. Used by permission. (www.Lockman.org). Scripture quotations marked (NIV) are taken from the *Holy Bible, New International Version®.* NIV®. Copyright © 1973, 1978, 1984 by International Bible Society. Used by permission of Zondervan Publishing House. All rights reserved.

Details in some anecdotes and stories have been changed to protect the identities of the persons involved.

ISBN 1-4000-7126-7

Copyright © 2005 by Bill Butterworth

Workbook materials and questions compiled by Elsa Kok.

Published in association with the literary agency of Alive Communications, Inc., 7680 Goddard Street, Suite 200, Colorado Springs, CO 80920.

Printed in the United States of America
2005—First Edition

10 9 8 7 6 5 4 3 2 1

Contents

Questions You May Have
About This Workbook

What will the *New Life After Divorce Workbook* do for me?

This workbook will help you walk through the healing process after divorce. You'll learn what it means to grieve, to lean on God, to grow, and to embrace new life. It's not an easy road you're embarking on, but it's well worth it. You have a future—an amazing future! It may not look like you expected it to, but God still has you in His hands. As you set your pain at His feet, He will heal the broken pieces and bring the new life you long for.

Is this workbook enough, or do I also need the book *New Life After Divorce*?

While this workbook is designed to work independently of the book, it's best to use them together. The actual book contains additional in-depth information and encouragement that will help as you move through this process.

The lessons look long. Do I need to work completely through each one?

This eight-lesson workbook is designed to walk you through the emotions associated with divorce. Some lessons won't apply to your particular situation (for example, the chapter on single parenting if you do not have children), so you may find it best to focus your time and discussion on some sections and questions more than others.

Should I work through the workbook with someone else?

It's always best to have someone to work with. Whether from a counselor, close friend, or small group, the feedback from others is invaluable. If you're nervous about sharing your innermost thoughts with a small group, at the end of each chapter some lighter questions for group discussion are listed. These will give you the opportunity to share as much or as little as you feel comfortable sharing.

Bottom line: This book is meant to help facilitate your healing after divorce—but God is the author of that healing. Talk to Him. Pray, asking Him to direct your thoughts and to bring people who will walk this journey with you. And as you do, may you discover fresh hope, new beginnings, and a future beyond what you can imagine.

Grieving the Loss and Accepting Your New Reality

SUGGESTED READING FOR THIS SESSION: chapter 1 from *New Life After Divorce*

This is a workbook you may not want to complete. In fact, you may even resent opening to this page. The life you imagined has not come to pass, and you're now working through to some distant "other side" where everything ought to be rosy. Maybe you're not feeling too rosy. Maybe the God-truth that all things work together for good for those who love Him (Romans 8:28) isn't offering you much comfort. That's okay. Before you can begin to move forward, you have to grieve the dream that was lost. Allow yourself the freedom to be angry, sad, and frustrated by the way things turned out. That's the exciting thing about these pages: the questions, the white space, the scriptures, the shared stories are meant to offer you a safe place to be real. And as you are real, as you begin to look toward a future that is different than you imagined, God will meet you. He will bring the hope and contentment that may seem elusive right now.

So let's go to Him first. Take a moment to pen a prayer to God's heart. Don't worry about sounding spiritual and "right." Just write your longing. What do you want Him to do through these pages? What do you need? Don't edit yourself. Just ask Him.

The Heartache

When the divorce happened, my world came crashing down. Some of my friends compared their divorces to being shot in the gut with a pistol. Mine felt like a one-two blast from a double-barreled shotgun. Not only was I blown away by the loss of the most treasured human relationship I had experienced, but the second shot blew me apart vocationally. Few groups wanted someone who was divorced to speak on marriages.

I felt like a Lexus dealer driving a Dodge Dart.

I did not work for six months. My debt grew every day. I felt like I was no good to anybody, and I struggled to get out of bed in the morning. I was a divorced, unemployed, sorry excuse for a man. So I did what any male would do in a similar situation.

I hid.

"No one is going to know my pain or embarrassment," I concluded. "I will go under cover." I became adept at dodging questions, avoiding eye contact, and changing the subject. People knew something was wrong, but I kept convincing myself they didn't. I was desperately lonely, deeply depressed, and committed to a classic case of denial. I lived each day waiting for the phone to ring, hoping my wife would say she wanted to get back together.

That phone call never came… 📖

1. Can you relate to Bill? What has been your emotional response to your divorce? Be specific, including ways you've coped that have been self-destructive (hiding, addictions, too much chocolate, rage).

Sometimes you may just need permission to feel. It could be that you've been told to be strong all your life, or you're trying to keep it together for the children, or you just haven't had the time. Here is your opportunity. Don't bypass the process of grief.

The healthy expression of grief can look different for each person and typically runs in stages. Much like grief over death, you may experience what Elisabeth Kübler-Ross described in *On Death and Dying* as the "stages of grief": denial, anger, bargaining, depression, and resolution/acceptance (see chapter 4 in *New Life After Divorce*). You may experience any one of these emotions—or all of them—in a single day! Or you may go back and forth along the spectrum of grief, thinking you have made progress only to discover that you're in denial again. You have to allow yourself the freedom to do so. Try any one of the following tools to help you process the multitude of emotions you're experiencing.

Write a letter to your ex-spouse. This is not a letter you have to send. It's to help you walk through all the emotion. Don't edit yourself. Don't attempt to justify, rationalize, be overly kind or outrageously cruel. Just write what you are feeling; reminisce about the good, vent over the bad. Write until you can write no more. Say good-bye. This doesn't have to be a one-time deal. Write as many letters as you need to write.

Write a letter to God. You may be angry with God over the divorce. Get it out. His shoulders are broad enough.

Verbally vent. If writing isn't the way you communicate best, set an empty chair in front of you. Imagine your ex-spouse there. (Don't worry. Close the shades, and the neighbors won't think strangely of you.) Pour out your heart and say good-bye.

Invite Jesus. For some of us, the memories of heartache in the marriage are overwhelming. Spend time in prayer, and invite Jesus into those situations. What would He do? What would He say? How would He comfort you, equip you, guide you? Ask Him for healing.

Seek professional help. We'll cover this more in a later chapter, but there is no shame in going to a counselor for help in the grieving process.

Attend a small group. Maybe you're using this workbook with a small group; this should be a safe place to process your feelings.

Call a friend. Again, we'll cover this in more detail later. We're supposed to help each other in the midst of the hurts of life. Call someone you know, cry on his or her shoulder, and yell if necessary. Don't lean completely on one person (that burden can be too much for an individual to carry), but don't be afraid to reach out.

Get physical. Walk, run, hike, or swim—daily if it helps. Take a kick-boxing class or learn tae kwon do. Exercise is an effective way to release negative emotion and clear cobwebs from your mind.

2. What is one practical step you are going to take to work through your emotions? Be specific and give yourself a deadline to get it done.

How Long Will the Pain Last?

Please realize that this is a process. You may start to feel content and abruptly get sideswiped by a painful moment. Life will come. Memories will come. Emotions will sneak in just as they did with Bill on his first solo Valentine's Day. He was attending a conference, and after dinner with a friend, he made his way back to the hotel room.

> 📖 I went back to my room, threw off my coat, and nearly choked myself taking off my tie. Throwing myself across the bed, I buried my head in the pillow and cried like a baby. The silent room intensified the sounds of my weeping. But inside my heart I was screaming at the top of my lungs: *Why did I have to be the one person in the whole stinking restaurant without a valentine? Why did it have to be my marriage that failed?* 📖

3. As you read about Bill's experience, can you relate? Explain.

4. Are there specific holidays or dates that you dread? Explain.

5. Do you believe that God will be there in those moments? Why or why not?

Read the following scriptures:

> Blessed are those who mourn, for they shall be comforted.
> (Matthew 5:4)

> Weeping may last for the night,
> But a shout of joy comes in the morning. (Psalm 30:5)

O may Your lovingkindness comfort me,

According to Your word to Your servant. (Psalm 119:76)

Bless the LORD, O my soul,

And forget none of His benefits;

Who pardons all your iniquities,

Who heals all your diseases;

Who redeems your life from the pit,

Who crowns you with lovingkindness and compassion;

Who satisfies your years with good things,

So that your youth is renewed like the eagle. (Psalm 103:2–5)

Therefore the LORD longs to be gracious to you,

And therefore He waits on high to have compassion on you.

(Isaiah 30:18)

6. What do these scriptures say to you about God's character in the midst of your grief?

7. These are promises for you. Are you able to take them as your own?
   Why or why not?

8. Do you ever feel guilty for the sadness you experience? Explain.

Bill shares:

> 📖 I still had many days of yearning for the past and the
> life I had planned for my family and me. That's not an evil
> thing. It's not falling off the wagon or regressing. It's real
> life. 📖

Give yourself some grace as you walk this journey. Some days you'll feel good. Other days you'll feel overwhelmed, angry, or sad. But as you seek God, as you look toward the future, as you say your good-byes and begin to accept this new reality, God will bring hope and healing.

> 📖 Part of achieving contentment comes from making
> progress. I make a little more every day. I now am grateful
> to God for bringing situations into my life that teach me
> truths I need to learn. I am developing a better under-
> standing of acceptance, contentment, and peace. 📖

ACCEPTING YOURSELF

As you take steps to grieve, you'll come to accept your new place in life. It won't be easy, but it will come. You are divorced, and you will be okay.

The more difficult part may be to accept yourself, to feel like you still have something to offer the world around you. As Bill shared in his story, he felt like a broken man, like a failure.

9. How do you feel about yourself now?

📖 Centuries ago King Solomon wrapped self-acceptance into one concise statement: "As he thinks within himself, so he is" (Proverbs 23:7).

You are what you think you are! If you think you're a no-good, dirty, rotten bum, that's the way you will live your life. Others will begin treating you that same way, because every signal you send them asks for that kind of treatment. Likewise, if I have a positive self-image, if I feel good about myself, this message will also translate to others, and they will respond appropriately.

Many of us struggled with low self-esteem *before* divorce entered our lives. The end of our marriages just feels like piling on. All of us deal with a level of insecurity, but some of us struggle more than others. As a child I viewed myself as the little fat kid that everyone else picked on. To my disservice, when I grew to be a man, I still tended to see myself the same way. Add a divorce to the equation, and I was convinced it all added up to a LOSER. 📖

10. Did you struggle with a specific insecurity before you married? Explain.

11. How has your divorce impacted your self-esteem?

Read the following scriptures:

> If I ascend to heaven, You are there;
> If I make my bed in Sheol, behold, You are there.
> If I take the wings of the dawn,
> If I dwell in the remotest part of the sea,
> Even there Your hand will lead me,
> And Your right hand will lay hold of me.
> If I say, "Surely the darkness will overwhelm me,
> And the light around me will be night,"
> Even the darkness is not dark to You,
> And the night is as bright as the day.
> Darkness and light are alike to You.
>
> For You formed my inward parts;
> You wove me in my mother's womb.
> I will give thanks to You, for I am fearfully and wonderfully
>   made;

Wonderful are Your works,

And my soul knows it very well. (Psalm 139:8–14)

But in all these things we overwhelmingly conquer
through Him who loved us. For I am convinced that nei-
ther death, nor life, nor angels, nor principalities, nor
things present, nor things to come, nor powers, nor
height, nor depth, nor any other created thing, will be able
to separate us from the love of God, which is in Christ
Jesus our Lord. (Romans 8:37–39)

12. According to these scriptures, how does God view you?

13. Are you able to take comfort from His Word? Why or why not?

If it's hard for you to accept yourself, try any of the following tools to help in the process.

Personalize scriptures. Take the previous scriptures, or find ones meaningful to you, and make them personal. Rewrite them, insert your name, and paste them where you will see them often. God's Word is living and active (Hebrews 4:12). He will use it to change your view.

Monitor your self-talk. Here's a simple rule. Don't say anything to yourself that you wouldn't say to a dear friend. Are you beating yourself up in your mind? Are you repeating messages that are harsh and condemning? Catch yourself. Keep a short account. Offer grace instead.

Look at your gifts. Take a piece of paper, and write down the gifts you have. Are you a good communicator? strong in organization? gifted in design? wise in solving problems? instinctive in looking out for others? Take a moment to assess your talents. Ask others for input if you get stuck.

Instead of the wounds, think of strengths. It's always easier to see how the divorce has robbed you. But what strength have you discovered that you didn't know you had? Be generous, be specific, be real.

14. Which of these steps can you take to remind yourself consistently of God's perspective?

DISCUSSION QUESTIONS

If you are working with a group, answer the following questions in the group.

15. Where are you in the grieving process of your divorce?

16. What was especially meaningful to you in this session? How has God met you?

17. How can the group pray specifically for you?

Leaning on God

SUGGESTED READING FOR THIS SESSION: chapters 2 and 11 from *New Life After Divorce*

Lynne was angry. And confused. She didn't understand what happened to the marriage she had poured so much of her heart and life into. Married nineteen years, she and her husband, Greg, shared the ups and downs typical of any couple. But their marriage was solid. They were active in church, she prayed for him faithfully, and she thought that overall they had something good.

Then Greg came to her one Friday night and coldly proclaimed that he didn't love her, hadn't loved her for a long time, and was leaving her. Lynne can still remember the way her heart pounded and the breath rushed from her lungs. She tried to reason with him, but he was unreceptive. He wanted nothing more to do with her. It was over, and Lynne had no say in the matter.

Lynne felt sucker-punched. At first she was angry with him, but the more she thought about it, she was angry with God. Why didn't God show up? Why didn't He hear her prayers? Why didn't God change Greg's heart?

It was enough to shake the very foundations of Lynne's faith.

1. Can you relate to Lynne? Explain.

2. Do you believe that God could have intervened in your marriage? Explain.

📖 So why did God allow your divorce to take place? For the same reason He allows murders, overeating, and gossip. Once Adam and Eve freely chose to disobey God in the Garden of Eden, sin entered the world. Even all these centuries later, you and I have our choice, or free will, to decide how we will live. 📖

3. If God radically intervened in every potential divorce, what would that say about our supposed free will?

So What Do We Do?

If you read Psalms, you discover what we can do with anger and frustration and even the feeling that God has abandoned us. Read some of what David shared:

> Why do You stand afar off, O LORD?
> Why do You hide Yourself in times of trouble? (Psalm 10:1)

> How long, O LORD? Will You forget me forever?
> How long will You hide Your face from me?
> How long shall I take counsel in my soul,
> Having sorrow in my heart all the day?
> How long will my enemy be exalted over me? (Psalm 13:1–2)

David was called a man after God's own heart (1 Samuel 13:14), and yet he freely expressed his fear and frustration. God must have loved David's passion and his honesty. If you read Psalms 10 and 13, you see that they start off in frustration and end in adoration. Something about the raw emotion of real relationship brought David back to the truth—that God is good, faithful, and trustworthy.

But to get to that point, David first had to release his anger. If you are angry, express it. If you are sad, call out to God. If you are frustrated, pour it out.

4. In the space below pour out your heart to God. Don't feel as if you need to create an emotion if you're not feeling it. But if you are in that place, let God know.

5. How does it feel to be honest with God? Explain.

God longs for real relationship with you. He longs to be there for you in the middle of all the emotion, because in the middle of it, He wants to show you things in His character that you can cling to.

He Is Your Comfort

> Indeed, the LORD will comfort Zion;
> He will comfort all her waste places.

And her wilderness He will make like Eden,

And her desert like the garden of the LORD;

Joy and gladness will be found in her,

Thanksgiving and sound of a melody. (Isaiah 51:3)

Then the virgin will rejoice in the dance,

And the young men and the old, together,

For I will turn their mourning into joy

And will comfort them and give them joy for their sorrow.

(Jeremiah 31:13)

6. What do these verses say about God's ability to comfort you? What does Scripture say that He will do with our sadness?

7. Do you believe that God longs to comfort you? Why or why not?

8. If you are in need of comfort, take a moment and ask it of God. Then watch to see how He responds. Keep your eyes open for the warm hug of a friend, a timely note, a beautiful sunset. Pen a prayer below if you need comfort today.

HE IS YOUR HEALER

On the Sunday before Christmas, I walked into the sanctuary of our church having no idea what was about to take place....

But something amazing was about to happen on that Sunday morning. The pastor began his sermon by reading a scripture: "The Spirit of the Sovereign LORD is on me, because the LORD has anointed me to preach good news to the poor. He has sent me to bind up the broken-hearted" (Isaiah 61:1, NIV)....

Meanwhile my pastor moved to the front of the pulpit and stood right beside the manger. He crouched down and said, "If you are in deep pain today, I invite you to leave your burden here in the manger. You don't need to physically get out of your seat and come down here. But in your heart, place all your brokenness on the straw of the manger. Remember, friend, Jesus Christ has come to mend that which is torn. He has come to bind up your broken heart." 📖

9. As you read of Bill's experiences and how God desires to bind up the brokenhearted, what is your response? Do you believe He is able to heal your wounds? Explain.

God is the ultimate healer. He takes what is broken and makes it whole. And as we love and pursue Him, He will use those broken pieces for our benefit. It's the miracle of the Father's hand. In His hand, the events in our lives that we are most ashamed of turn into our greatest strengths. He not only heals; He restores. He not only restores; He redeems. He is a miracle worker, and you are His miracle. As you say yes to Him, you will discover hope and healing beyond your wildest expectations. Will it be overnight? No. But in time, if you have allowed Him into the deep places of your life, you will be able to look back and be astounded by what He has done.

10. Can you imagine God using all your experiences? Why or why not?

11. Take a moment to write some thoughts to the One who loves you most. What would you like Him to do with all you are experiencing? Be specific. Be real. He wants to hear from you.

He Is Your Provider

One of the greatest struggles of divorce can be the financial hit. The level of income you once had now may be cut in half. If you were accustomed to being at home and caring for the kids, you may find yourself hunting for employment to sustain you. Or maybe both of you worked, and now both of you are struggling. Along comes child support or lawyer's fees or day-care expenses—all new since the divorce.

What can you do?

For starters, you can remember God's promises:

> He has given food to those who fear Him;
> He will remember His covenant forever. (Psalm 111:5)

> Therefore I tell you, do not worry about your life, what
> you will eat or drink; or about your body, what you will
> wear. Is not life more important than food, and the body
> more important than clothes? Look at the birds of the air;
> they do not sow or reap or store away in barns, and yet
> your heavenly Father feeds them. Are you not much more
> valuable than they? (Matthew 6:25–26, NIV)

12. What does God say about His ability to provide for you?

Adapting to a lower income level after a divorce can sometimes be a matter of learning to live more simply. You may not have the frills you once enjoyed, but God will take care of your needs. If you struggle with accepting a simpler lifestyle, or if you wonder how you will make it, use the space below to write your heart-felt concerns to God. Remember, He cares for you and is able to comfort you and provide for you. Talk to Him.

HE IS YOUR FATHER

What does it mean to trust that God is your Father in the midst of divorce? It means that not only will He comfort, strengthen, and provide; He will also teach. Just as a loving dad will teach his child what is right and wrong, your Father will do the same for you. If you draw close to Him, He will have the opportunity to show you where you are harboring anger, bitterness, or frustration. He will gently point out the rough edges that may have contributed to the divorce. He will open your eyes to ways you can love and serve your kids, your friends, or your ex-spouse. He will show you how to live through this with the grace and dignity that only He can bring.

He is enough. He is enough to see you through this—to be your refuge when you are weak, to comfort you when you are sad, to correct you when you are wrong, to hold you when you feel alone. He is your Father.

Read on:

> Blessed is the man whom You chasten, O LORD,
> And whom You teach out of Your law. (Psalm 94:12)

> My son, do not despise the LORD's discipline
>   and do not resent his rebuke,
> because the LORD disciplines those he loves,
>   as a father the son he delights in. (Proverbs 3:11–12, NIV)

> You have been a refuge for the poor,
>   a refuge for the needy in his distress,
> a shelter from the storm
>   and a shade from the heat. (Isaiah 25:4, NIV)

> I led them with cords of human kindness,
>   with ties of love;
> I lifted the yoke from their neck
>   and bent down to feed them. (Hosea 11:4, NIV)

13. What do these scriptures say about God as Father to you? Be specific to your situation.

14. Have you felt God's correction recently? Write about it.

15. Have you asked God to be your refuge? your teacher? your strength? Take a moment to write from your heart to Him now.

God Wants You to Seek Him

God is passionate for your future. He aches with your hurt and desires to bring healing. He is able to provide and strengthen, protect and comfort. Your role is to seek Him, pursue Him, and say yes to Him. As it says in Matthew 6:33, "Seek first His kingdom and His righteousness, and all these things will be added to you."

So what does that look like? Here are some practical tools that will help you as you desire to seek Him.

Spend time with Him. It sounds so simple, but time with God is often the first thing we set aside when life gets chaotic. Make sure you take time with Him—in the morning, in the evening—whenever you can.

Learn about Him. Go to God's Word and find out about His character. Sometimes we can doubt His goodness, or we learn about Him from other people and miss what He wants to teach us. Read His Word and take it personally.

Talk to Him. Be real. If you feel most comfortable on your knees, pray to Him there. Sit in your living room chair or write down your prayers in a journal—however you communicate best. Just communicate with Him. He wants to hear from you.

Celebrate Him. Take a walk, enjoy a sunset, allow yourself the joy of savoring a child's laugh. Notice Him in other people and in the world around you. As you celebrate Him, you will discover the most pleasant feeling: His celebration of you.

16. Which of these tools can you begin implementing right away?

17. Take a moment to talk to God about how you will reach out to Him. Set a time line and be specific.

DISCUSSION QUESTIONS

If you are working with a group, answer the following questions in the group.

18. How are you feeling about your relationship with God at this time? Explain.

19. What was especially meaningful to you in this session? How has God met you?

20. How can the group specifically pray for you?

Week Three

Calling on Friends

SUGGESTED READING FOR THIS SESSION: chapters 3 and 5 from *New Life After Divorce*

📖 Carrie's divorce was the most devastating event of her life. She loved Kevin and had trusted him since their first date in high school twelve years ago. To find out he had been carrying on multiple affairs during their ten-year marriage was the biggest shock Carrie had ever faced.… Soon the papers were filed, and the marriage was dissolved.

Carrie's response was overwhelming grief. "I would cry for hours," she recalled. "Then I would just stare straight ahead into space."…

Thankfully Carrie was connected to a group of women that met weekly. They were her friends, her prayer warriors; they were there for her.

"They helped in countless ways: baby-sitting, bringing

meals, inviting me to join their family activities when
Kevin had the kids—things like that. Before long, they
grew into a group that held me accountable for my
actions since I had no one else to look out for me.
They would be sounding boards as I talked about
struggles I had with Kevin or a problem that was devel-
oping with one of the children.... If I ever thought of
doing something crazy, I would see their faces in my
mind's eye. It kept me saner than I would have been
otherwise." 📖

BEING THERE

Within a group, Carrie was able to discover the varied benefits of friendship in
the midst of life's challenges. True friends offer companionship in the lonely
moments, help with practical needs, and challenge us spiritually. And we get to
return the favor by being there for them as well. So how does it happen? Let's
look at it together. As we approach each aspect of friendship, we'll talk about
some practical tools to equip you in this facet of your journey.

COMPANIONSHIP AND PLAY

You're in the middle of a war zone. Play may be the last thing on your mind.
But you need friends. You need moments where you think of nothing more
than pizza and football or popcorn and a good movie. Companionship and play
will crack open the door and allow some light into your world. You may not feel
up to spending time with friends, but it could be exactly what you need.

1. Do you currently have people in your life who are simply fun to be with? Write their names below and what you enjoy about them.

2. Take a moment to think about activities you enjoy. List them in the space below.

3. If you aren't taking any time to play, think of one person you can call to join you in one of the activities. Write his or her name in the space below and when you plan to call.

If you don't have friends that you can call for fun, here are some tips to cultivate those relationships.

Mingle. After church, stay an extra fifteen minutes and introduce yourself to two people you don't know (of your same sex). Ask about their interests. If you find a connection with someone, ask him or her to join you the next week for a hike, a movie—whatever the shared interest might be. Yes, it takes courage. And, yes, you can do it.

Join a club. There are all kinds of clubs available. If you like to read, join a book club. Connect with a community sports team. Learn scuba diving. Join the YMCA. Take dance lessons (line dancing doesn't require a partner). You may make all kinds of excuses for why you can't take the time. Don't listen to yourself. Get out there.

Join a singles group at church. You may not feel single, or you may think that joining a singles group means you are ready to date. It doesn't. Singles groups often offer activities that are fun and playful. Try a couple of them, and look for opportunities to build same-sex friendships.

4. Which of these ideas appeals to you? What will be your next step?

Listen to what God says about play, laughter, and friendship:

[There is] a time to weep and a time to laugh;
A time to mourn and a time to dance. (Ecclesiastes 3:4)

They drink their fill of the abundance of Your house;
And You give them to drink of the river of Your delights.
      (Psalm 36:8)

Behold, how good and how pleasant it is
For brothers to dwell together in unity! (Psalm 133:1)

A cheerful look brings joy to the heart. (Proverbs 15:30, NIV)

Isn't that the truth? A cheerful look *does* bring joy to the heart. You don't have to pretend that everything is okay; you don't have to put on a mask or go "play" when you feel like yelling or crying. But if you reach out and take a few steps to be around cheerful hearts, it might bring a smile to you when you least expect it.

5. Can you see the value of companionship and play even when you're hurting? Explain why it might be important for you personally.

HELP WITH PRACTICAL NEEDS

    📖 Say you're paying attention to what you are reading, and you decide to work on self-acceptance and healing from the Lord. Just when you think you are making progress in those areas, something unexpected hits your life. It can be anything from a crisis with one of your kids to a clogged bathtub. A painful conversation with your ex or a higher-than-anticipated credit-card bill. A low performance review at work or an attack by ten thousand ants in the laundry room. And because you are dealing with so much pain in the divorce proceedings, just the thought of more stress added to your life may seem like more than you can bear.

In the New Testament, the apostle Paul understood that concept. As if someone (could it have been a divorced person?) had come up to him and said, "I am so burdened down. This is more than I can bear," he wrote these words to the church on their behalf: "Bear one another's burdens, and thereby fulfill the law of Christ.… So then, while we have opportunity, let us do good to all people, and especially to those who are of the household of the faith" (Galatians 6:2, 10). 📖

6. Do you feel comfortable asking a friend for help? Why or why not?

Think about this:

> 📖 This is not a divorced-only club. No, I needed plenty
> of help from others when I was married. This is not an
> old-age issue. I needed help from others from my earliest
> memory as a child. It is not a cry of weakness, nor is it a
> mark of failure. We just need to understand and accept
> that if we are regular, garden-variety human beings trying
> to live in a way that pleases God, we are going to need
> assistance from other people. 📖

7. Do you acknowledge that we all need help occasionally? What do you
   need help with right now? Be specific.

You may have trouble asking for help. Here are some practical tips that may
open the door for you.

Barter strengths. Bill shares a story in chapter 3 of a gentleman who couldn't
cook. This man was frustrated because he was eating too many meals out and

gaining weight. Together, he and Bill thought up a unique solution: trade his skills at car maintenance for some cooking help. It worked.

8. What about you? What skills could you barter?

9. Get specific. Write down the names of those you could ask for help and what you could offer in return.

By asking for help, you're giving a gift. We all need to be needed. It feels good when a friend calls on us and we are able to help in a specific way. God designed us to help one another, and when we fulfill that role, we feel His delight. Don't think that your request for help is an imposition; it very well might be a blessing.

10. How do you feel when you are able to offer your specific strengths to help someone else?

11. Do you believe your request for help might be a gift to someone else? Explain.

Remember this is a season. You are asking for help in a specific season of your life. Two or three years down the road you could be in a position to offer someone else the same help and comfort. When we allow someone to comfort or help us, we often have a similar opportunity to pass it on. As Scripture shares, "Praise be to the God and Father of our Lord Jesus Christ, the Father of compassion and the God of all comfort, who comforts us in all our troubles, so that we can comfort those in any trouble with the comfort we ourselves have received from God" (2 Corinthians 1:3–4, NIV).

12. Does knowing that you may have the chance to help someone else make it easier to ask for help? Why or why not?

13. If you wrote down a specific need in question 7, now set a time limit to ask for help—and then ask!

ACCOUNTABILITY

   📖 Right after my divorce…one clear morning in May, I invited Alan to have a cup of coffee with me. "I am experiencing a void in my life," I admitted to my friend. "I don't have any men with whom I can be close. I need quality friendships, accountability, mental stimulation, and spiritual fellowship."

   We put our heads together and invited three other guys from our church to join us. And, voilà, over a strong cup of coffee our six o'clock breakfast accountability group—Alan, Fred, George, Duwaine, and I—was born....

These four guys became my best friends.... They would call me during the week to check in or to ask me to pray about something in their lives. But it's important to note that it didn't start out that way. It was risky to be so transparent at first. I didn't know these men that well when we began. But little by little we developed a special role in one another's lives.

The key purpose of the group was to provide accountability. As the months progressed, we became more open with each other and began sharing our concerns about our lives. 📖

We all need people in our lives who know the real scoop. They know our fears; they know our hurts; they know our temptations. These are the people who challenge us spiritually by asking the hard questions: Are you hiding in something? Are you avoiding God? How is that work project going? How can I pray for you?

14. How would you describe the value of accountability?

15. Are you accountable to anyone? Are there people who challenge you spiritually? Write their names and how they are a part of your life.

If you don't have someone who is watching your back spiritually, take a moment to read what God says on the topic:

Faithful are the wounds of a friend,
But deceitful are the kisses of an enemy. (Proverbs 27:6)

Oil and perfume make the heart glad,
So a man's counsel is sweet to his friend....
As in water face reflects face,
So the heart of man reflects man. (Proverbs 27:9, 19)

Iron sharpens iron,
So one man sharpens another. (Proverbs 27:17)

16. After reading these scriptures, how would you say God views accountability?

If you aren't accountable to anyone, these tools may help you start your own group.

Seek people of similar values but different experiences. Make sure to invite people based on their values and faith, but don't exclude people who are married, have different careers, or are older or younger. Different perspectives are often helpful.

Decide on a time. Pick a time that is convenient, either early morning or over lunch. Commit to being consistent (such as, every other Tuesday, every Wednesday).

Have an end in sight. Sometimes it's easier for people to commit if they know it's going to last a preset time—three months or sixteen weeks or whatever length works best for your group. Plan to reevaluate after that limit so people have the option of continuing or, if necessary, doing something different.

Pick a spot that's convenient. If you have single moms or dads in the group, offer to meet in their homes, or rotate locations to allow flexibility.

Guard against idle conversation. It's easy to lose an hour when you draw friends together. Give yourself a loose agenda that will give you the opportunity to ask questions, pray, and encourage each other in God's Word.

17. Are you willing to take steps to bring accountability to your life for the first time or to nurture it if you already have people with whom you're accountable? Explain how.

DISCUSSION QUESTIONS

If you are working with a group, answer the following questions in the group.

18. Share what you have learned about the value of friendship, especially in this season of your life.

19. What was especially meaningful to you in this session? How has God met you?

20. How can the group pray specifically for you?

Week Four

Seeking Wise Counsel

SUGGESTED READING FOR THIS SESSION: chapter 4 from *New Life After Divorce*

I am not spending one hundred dollars an hour to tell someone my problems, Shawna thought. She was driving home from church where she'd heard again how she needed to "get some help." Oh, she knew she was being a little harsh. Her friends were just trying to be supportive, but where would she get the money? And weren't friends just as good? Didn't going to a counselor mean that she had sunk so low that she now needed to pay someone to be her friend? Shawna fiercely wiped away the tear that coursed down her cheek.

"Mama?" Her daughter spoke up from the passenger seat. "Mama, are you okay?"

"I'm fine," Shawna said sharply.

"Mama? When are you going to stop being sad?"

Shawna just shook her head.

Moments later when they got home, she told the girls to go inside, and she stayed in the car, staring at her cluttered garage. Her daughter's question lingered in her mind. She'd been sad for so long. Before the divorce she had a hard time smiling because of the pain in their marriage. After the divorce she was no barrel of laughs, either.

"Maybe I need to talk to someone who knows about this stuff," she finally conceded. "Maybe it's time." Even as she said it, Shawna felt a little better. At least she was going to do something.

1. Do you relate to the sadness Shawna felt? Explain.

2. What is your perspective on counseling? Do you see it as something that could help you in your healing? Why or why not?

3. What would stop you from pursuing counseling for yourself?

Some people are embarrassed to share their problems with strangers. Others are concerned about the cost of counseling. And others have difficulty knowing whom they should trust as their counselor.

WHEN YOU'RE EMBARRASSED

📖 I went into counseling kicking and screaming. No, actually I went into counseling as a last resort because nothing else was working. After all, I had spent many years as a counselor myself; certainly I didn't need the kind of service I was offering others. Did I honestly believe I could heal myself? I attempted to pull the classic con on dear friends in order to get the name of a good referral in our area. I said, "I have a friend in my hometown who is having marital problems. Can you recommend a counselor for him?" I was as transparent as cellophane, but they played along with my charade and gave me the name of a counselor who helped me in tremendous ways.

Sitting in the waiting room at a counseling clinic felt like standing in a police lineup. I nervously went up to the receptionist's window, where I was forced to say my name aloud. No one waiting even bothered to look up, but I was mortified. I felt like saying, "Just hand me a sign to wear that says, 'I'm Bill Butterworth. I'm a very sick person, so you'll want to stay away from me.'" 📖

4. Can you relate to how Bill felt? If so, what is the truth? Is counseling really a bad thing? Is this about pride? Address your fear right here, and remind yourself of the truth.

It might help to know that God has some proverbs to share about seeking wisdom from others.

> The way of a fool is right in his own eyes,
> But a wise man is he who listens to counsel. (Proverbs 12:15)

He who walks with wise men will be wise,

But the companion of fools will suffer harm. (Proverbs 13:20)

Listen to counsel and accept discipline,

That you may be wise the rest of your days. (Proverbs 19:20)

5. According to these scriptures, what is God's counsel on pursuing help when you need it?

Here's one more thought that might be helpful:

📖 If you were driving in the desert and your car broke down, you'd gladly use your cell phone to call a mechanic. If you were in trouble with the Internal Revenue Service, you'd immediately call your accountant. If you were swimming in a pool of water thanks to a pipe that had burst in your home, you'd instantly call a plumber. The point is, when you are in a situation beyond your ability to handle, you call a professional.

It's the same with our lives. The mess that has been stirred up due to your divorce is potentially beyond your ability to decipher. Therefore, it makes great sense to consider seeing a counselor. 📖

6. Does Bill's statement make sense to you? Why or why not?

7. What is the difference between seeing a counselor and relying only on friends? Would you call just any friend if your car broke down or if you had problems with the IRS?

BUT I DON'T HAVE THE MONEY

This is a legitimate concern and one worth thinking about. Finances, especially after a divorce, can be a real deterrent to getting the help you need. But there are ways around this problem, and they begin with prayer. If you don't have the money for counseling right now, write down a prayer in the space that follows. Ask God. He has lots of money.

We talked about this in week 2, but let's review it. What does God have to say about his ability to provide?

> For this reason I say to you, do not be worried about your life, as to what you will eat or what you will drink; nor for your body, as to what you will put on. Is not life more than food, and the body more than clothing? Look at the birds of the air, that they do not sow, nor reap nor gather into barns, and yet your heavenly Father feeds them. Are you not worth much more than they? (Matthew 6:25–26)

> But seek first His kingdom and His righteousness, and all these things will be added to you.
> So do not worry about tomorrow; for tomorrow will care for itself. Each day has enough trouble of its own. (Matthew 6:33–34)

8. What is God saying?

God is more than able to provide for our needs. If you need counseling, He can take care of that, too. As you pray, think about the following options that you could pursue.

Call your church. If you attend a larger church, they may have a counselor on staff. Call and find out. See if they would be willing to reduce the cost. Often churches will grant a few free sessions, after which a reasonable fee will be expected. They may even provide for a payment plan.

Check your health insurance. Your health insurance may cover a certain number of sessions. Call and ask.

Ask about pro bono services. Most counselors will take a few patients for free. It never hurts to ask. Then later, when you have the resources, make sure to give back.

Look for God's answers. God may provide a temporary job to make some extra money, or He may remind you of your gifts (for example, in woodworking or painting) and encourage you to bring in more money using your talents.

Be alert to miracles. All the previous opportunities are ways that God works. He may also show up through an unexpected check in the mail, or He may provide in another area, freeing up finances.

However He works, He will work! Bring your need before Him, and see what He does.

9. Do you believe that God is able to meet your need? Why or why not?

10. Have you tried any of these tools to make counseling financially feasible? If not, which one appeals to you, and how can you take the next step?

BUT WHOM DO I ASK?

Once you make a decision to get help, it can be difficult to decide whom you should see. What if you pick the wrong person? How will you know if this counselor will help or hurt you? Those fears alone can be enough to stop you in your tracks. Don't worry. You can take some steps to help ensure the counselor is right for you.

Listen to what Bill writes in chapter 4:

> 📖 If you decide to visit a counselor, listing some expectations will help you choose one who is appropriate for your needs. For example, for me it was essential that the counselor be a Christian. I wanted to be assured that we held the same basic value structure so I would never be asked to violate my moral base. I have friends who have received wonderful help through non-Christian counselors, though I think that is a risky endeavor. I also have friends who had more extensive expectations of their counselors' qualifications. They needed reassurance of shared faith and also a clear understanding of their counselors' techniques and ways of integrating theology and psychology.
>
> I understand that choosing a counselor is a personal thing. All I am asking is that you don't let anything get in your way of that pursuit. 📖

11. If counseling is the next step for you, what are some of the priorities in your search (beliefs, location of office, price, etc.)?

Here are some other tools that may help you narrow the search.

Ask for referrals. If you are in a small group, ask others if they know of a good counselor who can help you with divorce-related issues.

Talk to your pastor. Call or visit your pastor. Ask if he can recommend anyone who is especially helpful to those working through divorce.

Check with large Christian organizations. Both New Life Ministries and Focus on the Family can refer you to Christian counselors in your area. You can reach New Life at www.newlife.com or at 1-800-NEW-LIFE and Focus on the Family at 719-531-3400, ext. 7700.

Know that you have a choice. You always have options. If you go for a visit and don't feel comfortable, you can choose not to return. You have to feel emotionally safe with whomever you expose your heart to. Stand firm in that.

12. Which tools would help you most as you seek a counselor? List specifically what you will do, and, if possible, give yourself a deadline.

DISCUSSION QUESTIONS

If you are working with a group, answer the following questions in the group.

13. Do you think counseling would be a valuable tool in your recovery? Why or why not?

14. What was especially meaningful to you in this session? How has God met you?

15. How can your group pray specifically for you?

Learning to Forgive ...and Get Along

SUGGESTED READING FOR THIS SESSION: chapters 6 and 8 from *New Life After Divorce*

Anna couldn't seem to sleep. She'd been trying for hours, but instead of rest, she found her eyes constantly wandering to the picture on her dresser. She hadn't been able to pack it away. The photo captured her and her husband of twenty-five years. The husband who no longer warmed his side of the bed. The husband who now, in fact, warmed someone else's bed. Anna felt the familiar bitterness surge within her. It'd been almost two years, but she couldn't seem to move forward. The bitterness instead continued to grow like a cancer. She knew she had to do something. Her dearest friend had gently encouraged her to forgive her ex, but the very thought made Anna sick to her stomach.

How could she forgive? Forgive the man who squandered their money? The one who ran off with another woman and left her to grow old alone? No, she didn't dare forgive. She simply couldn't.

1. Can you relate to Anna? Has your ex-spouse committed the unforgivable? Explain.

2. Why is it so hard to forgive? What keeps you from forgiving your ex-spouse?

WHY FORGIVE?

What does God say?

> And when you stand praying, if you hold anything against anyone, forgive him, so that your Father in heaven may forgive you your sins. (Mark 11:25, NIV)

Therefore, as God's chosen people, holy and dearly loved, clothe yourselves with compassion, kindness, humility, gentleness and patience. Bear with each other and forgive whatever grievances you may have against one another. Forgive as the Lord forgave you. And over all these virtues put on love, which binds them all together in perfect unity. (Colossians 3:12–14, NIV)

3. What is God saying about forgiveness in these scriptures?

4. What does it say to God when we staunchly refuse to forgive?

God doesn't ask us to forgive others as some cosmic joke. He doesn't do it to be mean. He has a reason. When we don't forgive, we lose. We suffer. God can't move in our lives to forgive and help us because we're stuck in bitterness. As Bill shares in chapter 6, without forgiveness we stay stuck in the past, we feel more alone, we risk emotional and physical illness, and we actually give control of our emotions to the very person who hurt us.

5. Can you see how lack of forgiveness has robbed you of life? Explain.

6. How do you think your life would change if you were able to forgive your ex-spouse?

HOW DO WE FORGIVE?

It might be helpful to look first at what forgiveness is NOT.

Forgiving is not forgetting. When we forgive our former spouses, it does not mean we will automatically forget all the hurt and pain that resulted from our marital breakdowns. That's unrealistic.

Forgiving is not a feeling. We choose to forgive whether we feel like it or not. We don't have to feel warm fuzzies in the process; we are simply choosing to release our exes from the relational debt they created by their actions.

Forgiving is not fair. Saying "I forgive you" doesn't seem fair in view of all the sleepless nights, the cheating, the lying, and the physical, emotional, and mental abuse. It wasn't really fair that Jesus had to die on the cross for all we did wrong, but He did.

Forgiving is not approval of the offender. These are two separate things. We can forgive the offenders without condoning their behavior.

Forgiving is not extending trust. Trust must be earned, but forgiveness is a gift made by choice. Trusting someone who hurt you may not be beneficial, but forgiveness is.

Forgiving is not easy. It requires a certain degree of strength, discipline, and courage. But it is worth it, because forgiveness releases us to live.

7. As you read over this list, does it clarify what forgiveness is NOT? Do you get stuck on any one issue? Write it here.

Now let's look at what forgiveness is.

Forgiveness is a choice to let go. We're wiping the slate clean. We can't wipe the feelings away, but we are choosing not to hold history against our former spouses. This act, in and of itself, frees us. We no longer look for ways they must pay the debt. We no longer look for ways they are adding to the debt they owe. Instead, we're choosing not to keep a record of wrongs, because that kind of relational accounting robs us of life and joy.

It's letting go. Not all at once, but every day, every moment if needed—until it is done.

8. Does this definition of forgiveness help or hinder you? Explain.

Once we know what forgiveness is and what it is not, we can move on to the actual process of forgiving. Here are some tools that may help you along the way.

Make it part of your morning. Actually speaking forgiveness on a daily basis will help. You don't have to say it to your ex, but say it in your quiet time. Consciously forgive him or her on a daily basis.

Keep a short account. Bitterness can creep in and consume a day (or even a week) before we know it. Keep a short account of your feelings, and the moment you start dwelling on the wrong, bring it to God's feet and leave it there.

Find safe outlets to get it out. At times we may need to vent so we can move through an emotion. Develop friendships with safe people who will allow you to vent and afterward will direct you to forgiveness.

Write it out. Write a letter detailing the offenses and offering forgiveness. This is not a letter you need to send.

Go to Scripture. Remind yourself of the far greater debt we owe God, and He wiped the slate clean. Considering that kind of magnificent grace tends to soften us.

9. Do any of these tools appeal to you? Which one can you incorporate in your daily process of forgiveness? How do you think it will help?

10. After reading through this last section, do you believe forgiveness is possible? Why or why not?

Your ex-spouse may not be the only one you need to forgive. Bill suggests several other people who may need your forgiveness.

Yourself. Have you forgiven yourself for the role you played in the divorce? Sometimes we can be harder on ourselves than we have ever been on others.

> God promises me personal forgiveness for all the
> things I have done wrong, and that includes my part in
> the destruction of my marriage. On the outside, people

may see me as the innocent party or the real villain, but
in God's eyes I am forgiven in either case if I confess my
sin to Him and ask for His forgiveness. So if God forgives
me, I need to get with the program and forgive me as
well. 📖

Any third parties. Yes, God even calls us to forgive a third party who may have
intervened in the marriage.

Others. Are you holding others responsible? A counselor? pastor? child? parent or in-law?

11. Can you think of anyone other than your ex-spouse whom you have
    yet to forgive (including yourself)? Write the names here.

12. What can you do to start the process of forgiving these individuals? Be
    specific.

Forgiveness is divine. It's nearly impossible to do it on our own. Let's enlist God's help in the process. Pen a prayer here, exposing your heart and calling out to Him, and then watch for ways He is working in your life.

AND GETTING ALONG...

In some respects I consider myself an expert in dealing with a former spouse, if you qualify for expert status by making every mistake known to man. In my early days of dealing with my divorce, I was a sad case indeed.

I went through a phase where I was one angry dude. I got to the point that I couldn't speak to my former wife in a subdued, calm voice. Even when we spoke on the phone, I lashed out in angry rampages about how I viewed the state of our dissolution. Sometimes I hung up the phone with such force I fully expected the receiver to shatter.

Of course, there were other phases. The anger could be replaced with the sad, desperate pleas of a shattered man. "Won't you please consider getting back together? We can make it work this time, I just know we can."

Pleading would lead to begging, and begging would lead to the total loss of self-dignity.

The zombie mode was another interesting facet of dealing with my ex. I would see her in order to take care of some business matter or pick up or drop off the kids, and I would exhibit nothing more than a blank stare. "Are you okay?" she would ask.

"Whatever," I would reply with all the feeling of bituminous coal. Blink and stare, blink and stare—a very unhealthy, nonwinsome pattern of behavior.

Add cynicism, disrespect, and other ungodly behavior and you could pretty much fill out the package known as Bill Butterworth in my early days of divorce. 📖

13. Can you relate to Bill? What types of reactions have you exhibited to your former spouse?

Right after the divorce it's almost impossible to be chipper and friendly when you run into your spouse. But there are definite ways to ease the stress and anxiety that may be tied to your interactions. Bill talks about them in chapter 8; we'll summarize them here.

Establish healthy boundaries. You were once one with this individual. It can be hard not to act like it anymore.

📖 Since you're not married to this person anymore, you are not responsible for his or her behavior. You don't need to fix her flat tire if that's the only reason she's called you in the last ten weeks. You don't need to send him frozen casseroles with the kids because you know when he's by himself he eats nothing but junk. You're single again, dear friend. And part of what that means is that she will ultimately have to learn how to take care of herself in automotive emergencies. And he will either start eating healthier or face the consequences at his next doctor's appointment.

And it's not your fault in either case. 📖

Helping each other is not a bad thing. It's fine to offer a casserole or help with a flat tire—if your motive is checked. But when the boundaries are fuzzy and you feel overly responsible, it's time to remind yourself that you are no longer married. Otherwise, getting along with your former spouse will only get stickier as those boundaries remain undefined.

14. Do you have trouble maintaining healthy boundaries in your divorce? Explain.

15. What can you do to establish healthy boundaries?

I will do my best to move on with my life. Getting along postdivorce is really only possible when both parties have let go and moved on. Otherwise, any kind of contact and relationship becomes painful and full of stress.

16. Do you feel as though you have moved on? If not, why?

If your divorce is recent and the pain is still fresh, don't worry about it. Give yourself some time. If, however, it has already been several years, it might be a good idea to ask God to show you what you are holding on to.

I will honor the financial arrangements. If you are responsible for paying spousal support and/or child support, honor your agreement. Pay the full amount and pay on time. If you receive spousal support and/or child support, honor your agreement. Don't continually nag, whine, or renegotiate for more money.

17. Are you having trouble honoring the financial arrangements made during your divorce? If so, what can you do to improve in this area?

See the big picture. Bill shares the story in chapter 8 of how he and his wife ended up having lunch with his ex-wife and the kids. The scenario was uncomfortable at first, but as they ate together, Bill could see how animated and engaged the kids had become. It meant a lot to them that Bill and his former wife were able to put aside their differences to enjoy a meal together. You may not be able to picture yourself in this scenario in the near future, but it could still be possible. If you will see each other at family events in the future (graduations, weddings, etc.), it makes all the difference if you can take steps to get along. You don't have to love it, you don't even have to like it, but by making the effort, you can offer the kids a sense of security and joy.

18. Is it hard for you to imagine a day like the one Bill shared with his ex? Explain.

Obviously, there are scenarios where even civil reconciliation is impossible. If this is your story, don't feel guilty or overwhelmed. There are simply times when a former spouse is completely unwilling, a danger to be around, or too far away. If this is your situation, please know that you don't have to accomplish the impossible. If it can't be done, you can still find comfort and companionship in the One who loves you most. You are not alone!

Discussion Questions

If you are working with a group, answer the following questions in the group.

19. Where do you need to take some additional steps—learning to forgive or getting along? Explain.

20. What was especially meaningful to you in this last session? How has God met you?

21. How can the group specifically pray for you?

Week Six

Single Parenting

Suggested reading for this session: chapter 7 from *New Life After Divorce*

📖 My alarm shrieks a reminder of all that needs to be done before the kids leave for school. I wake the high schoolers first, then I begin an assembly line of brown-bag lunches lined up on the kitchen counter as I wait for the Starbucks to brew. About the time the pot's gushing sound signifies the cycle is complete, abuse begins.

"Peanut butter and jelly again?"

"Can't we have Twinkies instead of an apple just once?"

It's not fair to be subjected to this sort of mistreatment before caffeine is flowing through the body's system.

"Knock it off, you guys!" I bark back. "Everyone be quiet and eat your breakfast."

"You bought the gross cereal again, Dad. It tastes like tree bark."…

"We're out of here, Dad," they yell. One by one, loud voices depart, leaving me to the quiet of an empty house.…

I pick up the cereal bowls left on the counter and head for the dishwasher. But it hasn't been run! "They can't pour a little detergent in a hole, close a door, and press a button?" I mutter to no one in particular. 📖

Bill later describes the end of his day:

📖 I help the younger ones get ready for bed, tuck everyone in, turn out the lights, and stumble wearily back to my own bedroom. As I pull back the covers, a small piece of paper on the pillow catches my eye. My eyes fill with tears as I read a note from my daughter: "Dear Dad: Thank you for everything you do for the boys and me. I know we don't express it enough, but we sure do realize it. Thanks, Dad. I love you!!" 📖

1. Do your days look anything like the one Bill described? Have you received a note like his? Write about it.

Whether you've received acknowledgment from your children or not, it's important that you know something: God is proud of you. Your job as a single parent is hard. You may be tired and overwhelmed. You may be irritable and grumpy sometimes. You may yell when you need to smile, or laugh when you need to be serious. And maybe you're too hard on yourself. Friend, you need to know that in the middle of it all, Someone notices. And Someone cares. God notices. He cares. And He wants to be there for you.

O taste and see that the LORD is good;
How blessed is the man who takes refuge in Him!
(Psalm 34:8)

How priceless is your unfailing love!
Both high and low among men
find refuge in the shadow of your wings. (Psalm 36:7, NIV)

Sing to God, sing praise to his name,
extol him who rides on the clouds—
his name is the LORD—
and rejoice before him.
A father to the fatherless, a defender of widows,
is God in his holy dwelling.
God sets the lonely in families. (Psalm 68:4–6, NIV)

When I remember You on my bed,
I meditate on You in the night watches,
For You have been my help,
And in the shadow of Your wings I sing for joy.

My soul clings to You;
Your right hand upholds me. (Psalm 63:6–8)

2. God is there for you. Do you believe it? He delights in your desire to be a good parent. Can you feel it? Why or why not?

If you have trouble feeling God's care for you, use the following space to make one of the previous scriptures personal. Put your name at the start, and turn it into a personal note of encouragement.

WORKING WITH OTHERS

God is not your only ally. In addition to seeking encouragement from Him, you can work with other parents to ease your load and stress level. Think about some of these timesavers that could help you out.

Carpool. Don't be afraid to ask other parents for carpool ideas. If you spend a lot of your time driving kids from here to there, seriously consider asking some parents to share the load. There are a lot of other parents who would benefit as well—married and single.

Baby-sitting. Get a baby-sitter so you can have some time away. Guilt will often keep single parents from getting childcare, but the truth is, you will function better if you take the time. If cost is a consideration, try the local YMCA for parents' night out events, check with a college for willing early-education students, or ask the youth group at church for volunteers.

Share meal duties. Take note if there are other single parents in your neighborhood. Why not alternate meal responsibilities and have dinner together?

Enlist children. As soon as your kids are old enough to wash dishes or do laundry, give them the chance to do so. Don't overwhelm them, but it's good for them to know that they are contributing to their home environment.

3. Are any of these tools viable options for you? Which ones, and how will you make them happen?

4. What other creative ways can you think of for getting help and sharing the load of single parenting? Write them here. (If you get together with a group, be sure to share them!)

Helping the Kids

As you grow in the realization that you are not alone, and as you incorporate ways to ease the load, you can focus more energy on your children's needs. They may be assuming that the divorce was their fault.

5. Have any of your children indicated that they feel they are to blame? Explain.

Take your children's feelings seriously. Sit with them and hold them close. Tell them as many times as they need to hear it that the divorce had nothing to do with them. Remember, kids might not even share the fact that they are feeling responsible. Let them know they are not to blame whether they express that concern or not.

Let's talk a little more about where your children are emotionally.

6. How are your children coping with the divorce? Be specific for each child.

7. What strengths in your children are you excited to see? What weaknesses concern you?

There are tools to help you parent your child through this season. Bill spoke of them in chapter 7, and we'll summarize them here.

Don't treat your child like a parent. Without realizing it, we can realign the family structure to put one child in the role of the missing parent. We might lean on that child for support, ask for advice, or even assign more chores than is reasonable. Guard against that by letting your child remain a child. Give him or her opportunities to play or be silly, and don't turn the child into your confidant.

Don't use your child as a messenger. Don't send messages to the other parent through your child. Keep your communication separate.

Don't ask your child to be a spy. "What's your mother doing?" may sound like an innocent question, but it's not. First of all, it's none of your business what she is doing, and, second, the question places your son or daughter in an awkward position. The child may know that the answer will hurt you, so he or she must then decide whether to tell you or to lie about it.

Don't speak negatively of the other parent. Speaking critically of someone benefits no one. Kind words will come back to benefit you, just as harsh words will come back to bite you. So be positive.

Don't let your child manipulate you. Your child's regular testing of limits will include pushing every button he or she knows how to push in order to get the desired result. If you see your little ten-year-old sad and despondent over life's circumstances, try to ascertain if it's genuine. Many a kid has scored a shiny new bike as a result of manipulating the parent!

8. Have you found yourself falling prey to any of these issues? Explain.

9. Can you see how these things could damage your child? In what ways? Be specific.

So what can you do? The best gift you can give your child is stability. By being in control, maintaining love and discipline, and avoiding the pitfalls, you give your child a strong foundation in your single-parent home. We gave you a list of don'ts earlier. Here is a list of dos from chapter 7.

Establish and follow a routine. Knowing what is happening at what time and who is responsible for what task can unlock the door to harmonious family life.

Celebrate special days. Make holidays and birthdays special. Consider throwing celebrations for smaller achievements, too, just because.

Regularly affirm your children's worth. Don't just affirm their accomplishments, but give them hugs and attaboys just for being who they are.

Affirm their relationship with their other parent. You may need to muster up your best acting skills to acknowledge that your children still love their other parent. It will do your child a world of good if you can even point out a few positive traits. Remember, they are related by blood to that person.

Maintain boundaries. Intentionally pursue your own life. There are places and times that are for you alone, without the children, just as there are times and places for the kids without you. That's healthy. Setting up strong boundaries allows each of you to maintain a healthy, unique identity without being overly dependent on someone else.

10. Do any of these tools resonate with you? Which one can you incorporate with your kids? How will you do it? Be specific.

FINDING MENTORS

In addition to what you are able to do, recruit others to invest in your children as well. Single parents all over the country share one cry: mentors. They long for mentors for their children, for other adults willing to come alongside and instruct, teach, and support their kids. If you have the same desire, here are some practical tips.

Get on your knees. Pray hard and pray often. God hears your cry.

11. Pen a prayer in the space that follows. Be specific.

Don't expect one person to do it all. Even if God sent you the perfect mentor, he or she couldn't be everything to your child. You will probably find it necessary to seek out mentors who can mold your children in different ways.

12. Name three areas in which your child would benefit from being mentored.

Look to the church. Each Sunday look around for people who could be mentors. Ask God to direct you to the right ones.

13. If possible, name three people who might match up to the areas you listed in question 12.

14. What is your next step in getting a mentor for your child? Be specific.

Remember, you are not alone. God is standing with you. He can bring others to surround you. He is crazy about you, and He loves your kids even more than you do. You won't get all of this perfect. That's okay. You weren't a perfect parent when you were married, either. Where you are not perfect, God is. And He can do the same thing with your child's story that He is doing with yours. He can take the broken pieces and fashion them into strength. He can take the hurts and build compassion. He is the Master Artist, and as you bring your children to His feet, He will scoop them up, hold them close, and comfort them. That's who He is.

Discussion Questions

If you are working with a group, answer the following questions in the group.

15. What is your greatest concern as a single parent? Explain.

16. What was especially meaningful to you in this last session? How has God met you?

17. How can the group pray specifically for you?

Week Seven

Dating

SUGGESTED READING FOR THIS SESSION: chapter 9 from *New Life After Divorce*

David straightened his tie and ran his fingers through his hair. He tried to imagine how his date would see him. Would she think he was handsome? He puffed out his chest and turned to the side. He'd been working out. Was it obvious?

"Dad, what are you doing?"

It was his daughter, Angela, a teenager with eyes like a hawk and curiosity to match.

"She's going to love you, Dad. How could she not?"

Love me? David thought. *No, not quite ready for that. Smitten maybe? Yeah, that'd be okay.*

"I'm not going for love." He smiled. "I'm going for smitten."

Angela laughed. "Oh, she'll definitely be smitten. You're very handsome."

David couldn't help but find the conversation surreal. Dating encouragement from his daughter? Wasn't it supposed to be the other way around?

It felt even more surreal as he talked with her about curfews. "I'll be home by eleven, okay? So don't worry and don't wait up."

She came over and straightened his tie one more time. "I'll be fine, Dad. Just have fun."

He caught his own anxious look in the mirror. Fun? Was all this supposed to be fun? Somehow it didn't feel like it. He took a deep breath. Was he even ready for this? Had enough time passed?

Maybe he wasn't as ready as he'd thought.

1. As a single person again, have you thought about dating? How do you feel about the process? Do you think you're ready? Explain.

READY? OR NOT?

Sometimes it can be difficult to figure out if you're ready to date. You might feel lonely and think, *Maybe this is a good time.* You might meet someone interesting and wonder if God is sending you a signal. Or people you love might be setting you up and encouraging you to get "back into the game." Maybe you have tried it already, dipped your toe in the water, and discovered it's a bit too scary. So how can you know whether you're ready?

There are some practical ways to find out if you are ready to date, but the best way to know is to ask God. Pen a prayer to Him in the space that follows, and ask Him to use the following pages to help you discern where you are.

Before you are ready to date, you should have some things settled in your own heart. Bill talks about them in chapter 9; we'll explore them here.

Have You Grieved?

It's just as we talked about in week 1 of this workbook: you need to take time to grieve before you can move on to a healthy relationship. Grief is not an event; it's a process. It happens over time as various issues come to light. Although you don't have to be completely finished grieving before you move on, you will benefit if you have worked through the bulk of your grief. Here are some tools to help you figure out where you are in the grieving process.

Ask a close friend. Check with people you trust. Do they believe you have walked through the sadness? Ask them honestly, and listen to their response.

Do a time check. If it's been a month since your divorce, don't even think about it! Give yourself time to heal and grow through this. Many suggest a two-year time period, depending on the length of your marriage. Ask a counselor or trusted friend who knows your situation.

Stay in tune with your feelings. If you're still fighting intense anger, sadness, or frustration, don't move on to dating. Be aware of what you're feeling.

Seek God's direction. God knows your needs. He knows your desires. He also knows if you are ready to date. Ask Him, and watch for His answer.

2. After reading through these items, where do you believe you are in the grieving process? Do you believe you have moved far enough through it to start dating? Explain.

Are You Grounded in Christ?

One of the temptations after divorce is to look for someone who will assure us that we are lovable. If you've felt the rejection that typically accompanies a broken marriage, it's easy to wonder whether something is wrong or missing in you. This is the perfect setup for rushing into another relationship. Someone finds you handsome or beautiful; someone looks at you with a smile in his or her eyes. It can be easy to throw caution to the wind and wrap yourself up in this person who believes in you.

The problem comes when reality sets in and you discover that you've fallen for someone simply because he or she fell for you, not because you love that person as an individual.

How can you prevent this? Find your hope and identity in Christ. Spend time with Him; read in His Word about how much He loves you. Ask Him to show you what you mean to Him so you won't be tempted to run to someone else. Invest in your relationship with Him through prayer, Bible study, and accountability.

Once you find your identity in God's love for you, then you can begin looking for an outside relationship without being dependent on it. God's love will free you to love the people He sets in your life for who they are, not for how they love you in return.

3. Describe your relationship to Christ in this season.

4. Do you feel grounded in His love for you? Why or why not?

5. We covered some tools for connecting to God in week 2 of this workbook. Have you been able to implement them? What can you do to continue building your relationship with Him? Be specific.

Establish Your Own Identity

It's important to have other things going on in your life. Hopefully, you enjoy your work, have a few hobbies, and engage in opportunities to serve. If you don't, you may tend to wrap your whole identity around the newest love interest. This is dangerous for you and for whomever you're dating. Make sure you have your own life. A good gauge is to do a desperation check. Do you feel you have to go out with someone to be happy? If so, be honest with yourself, back up, and strengthen other aspects of your life.

6. Do you have interests outside of finding a dating relationship? Talk about them here.

7. What is your desperation factor? Would you be okay if you didn't date for a while? Explain.

Develop Friendships

Friendships matter. A good friend will be able to offer companionship and opportunities for play. If you don't have good friends, you may lean too heavily on your dating relationship to meet all your needs. Friends are also wonderful for helping you realize potential blind spots. They can help guide you in your dating so you don't fall into a relationship that is wrong for you.

8. Do you have friends who meet your needs in different ways? Write them below.

9. Do you have friends who are willing to be honest with you? If you were rushing into something unhealthy, would they tell you? Write their names below. You may need to give a few people permission to say those things if necessary. If that is the case, write their names, and give yourself a schedule to make those requests.

Know Your Nonnegotiables

What is important to you? Certain things are not negotiable in a marriage relationship. Maybe you need someone who is good with kids because you have several. Perhaps you need someone who is thinking about going into the ministry because that is your heart's desire and calling. Or maybe you want to be with someone who will enjoy travel or the outdoors or Oreo cookies. Because of your experience in marriage, you likely have a good idea of what you need and what you can't tolerate.

10. Write down five things you know you want in a future mate.

11. Share these things with your friends, and ask them to remind you of what you want. Are you willing to stand by your list? Explain why it's important to do so.

12. Write down potential consequences of ignoring your list. (Review it occasionally in case you're tempted to ignore what you need!)

BEING IN RELATIONSHIP

Once you are ready to begin dating, there are some tools that can help you date in a way that honors God and is fruitful. Think on these things.

       📖 *Go slowly.* Proceeding with caution in the world of dating sounds so simple, so basic that it's almost insulting to include it as a point to ponder.

Be insulted. Ponder it.

Speed dating is a tendency everyone faces. We are tempted to move a relationship ahead at the speed of light. 📖

13. Do you tend to move quickly in dating? What steps can you take to guard yourself from this potential?

14. Describe the progression of your relationship with your former spouse. What did you learn from that situation?

Be Honest. It could be that your marriage was not a safe place to expose your heart. Maybe you were honest about something, and he or she blew up in the face of it. Maybe you want to be a knight in shining armor, so you don't want to shatter her image of you with a breakup. Or perhaps you're afraid to hurt his feelings, so you keep holding on. Regardless of the circumstances, being honest is always the best course of action. If you tend to shade the truth, you probably already know this about yourself. Maybe it's time to make a change.

15. Are you able to be honest in your relationships? Why or why not? What do you have to lose by being honest?

16. What steps can you take to strengthen this core ingredient of successful relationships? Be specific.

Stay pure. One of the most difficult issues of a dating relationship after divorce is the matter of purity. When you have already had an intimate physical relationship, expressing yourself physically can seem like the most natural thing in the world, while purity can feel most unnatural. Maintaining purity is not just an issue for teens and college students; purity is relevant at any stage of life. God designed sex for the marriage bed, because it physically draws a husband and wife together as one. If you date someone, sleep together, and then break up, the resulting spiritual and emotional wounds are far from the best plan God has for you. You've bonded at a spiritual level, and breaking that bond can break your heart also.

Listen to what God says in His Word:

> For this reason a man shall leave his father and his mother,
> and be joined to his wife; and they shall become one flesh.
> (Genesis 2:24)

17. What is the order of events depicted in this scripture?

> Now to the unmarried and the widows I say: It is good for
> them to stay unmarried, as I am. But if they cannot con-
> trol themselves, they should marry, for it is better to marry
> than to burn with passion. (1 Corinthians 7:8–9, NIV)

18. If it is better to marry than to burn with passion, what is Paul saying about the expression of passion and when it's appropriate?

> It is God's will that you should be sanctified: that you should avoid sexual immorality; that each of you should learn to control his own body in a way that is holy and honorable. (1 Thessalonians 4:3–4, NIV)

19. What is God's will for purity in your life?

As you've worked through this chapter, you may have discovered that you are ready to begin dating. If so, that's wonderful! Take it slow, follow God's direction, and maintain purity. If you're not ready, don't hesitate to stand firm in that. You have all the freedom in the world to take the time you need. Listen to what God might be whispering, and allow yourself to feel good about where you are.

DISCUSSION QUESTIONS

If you are working with a group, answer the following questions in the group.

20. Do you believe you are ready to enter the dating world? Do you have hesitations? Write your thoughts here.

21. What was especially meaningful to you in this last session? How has God met you?

22. How can the group specifically pray for you?

Week Eight

Change and New Beginnings

SUGGESTED READING FOR THIS SESSION: chapters 10 and 12 from *New Life After Divorce*

Elizabeth could almost taste her fear as she locked the door of her home. She hated being alone. Her divorce was final two months ago, but she still couldn't get used to her new role as a single. Her heart pounded, just as it did every night when she locked the door. She was afraid. Not just afraid of things that go bump in the night, but afraid of what the future might hold. How would she survive? What was she going to do? It all felt surreal, and she had no idea what to do with the waves of emotion that overwhelmed her.

Elizabeth had never been big on change anyway. Taking the steps to leave an abusive marriage had sapped all her strength. Sometimes she thought she should have stayed with Stan. At least with him, she knew what to expect. But now, on her own, she wasn't sure what lay ahead and if she would be able to handle it. She didn't like being alone, didn't like facing the unknown.

Change, she thought, *is for the birds.*

Across town, Jack wasn't much different. While he handled his resistance to change a little differently, he was as scared as anyone else. Oh, he didn't often admit it, but when Lucy left, his world dropped out from beneath him. Coming home to an empty house was the worst. He often worked late just to avoid the sound of his own footsteps echoing through the house. If he'd been watching, he would have seen the divorce coming. But he hadn't wanted to see it, and now he was alone. He missed his wife. He missed the dogs. He missed the shared meal at the end of the day, the conversation. This new place in life was too unpredictable, too different from all that he'd known. And he didn't like it.

Change, he thought, *is for the birds.*

1. Can you relate to Elizabeth and Jack? Describe your feelings as you think about this new season as a single-again.

📖 We are in a far better place if we choose to accept change, since it's happening whether we accept it or not!

> Making friends with change can revolutionize our lives,
> not only assisting us in processing our divorces but giving
> us tools for all kinds of life issues. 📖

2. Can you see how understanding and embracing the process of change might help you in other areas of your life as well? Explain.

Understanding Change

Before we can accept change in our lives, it is helpful to understand the process involved. Bill talks about that in chapter 10, and we'll review a summarized version here.

Calm. Life is cruising along. It might not be all we desire, but we know what to expect. The days are orderly and scheduled.

Control. We typically feel in control when all is going according to plan.

Crisis or Choice. Life comes. We're faced with change. Sometimes the change comes by choice or decision; other times it is forced upon us with little or no advance warning in the form of a crisis. Either way, things are anything but calm, and we are no longer in control.

Confidence. As we walk through this new development, we discover strengths that maybe we didn't know we had. While we may have gotten stuck or grumped a little, at least we are still standing and are moving through it.

Character. As our confidence increases, it sinks into our character. We have walked through something difficult or life altering, and we are now the stronger for it. Our character has deepened; we're more resilient, better equipped, tougher.

Calm. And back we come to calm waters, moving forward normally and with a few more learning experiences under our belts.

3. When you read through this process of change, where do you place yourself? Are you in crisis mode? Are you moving toward confidence, or have you already seen the effects of this change on your character? Explain.

Don't be too hard on yourself if you are still in the crisis mode of change. Chances are you picked up this workbook because you are hurting and want to walk through to the other side. You're doing exactly what you should be doing. Confidence and transformed character lie ahead. Keep walking, keep working. You're getting there!

Why Is It So Hard?

It's scary to move from one place in life to another, especially going from married to single. This is a change you didn't expect. You didn't get married thinking you would have to revert to singleness. So not only is this change frustrating because of the nature of change, it's also overwhelming because it wasn't supposed to happen. Let's take it one step at a time by looking at some of the common fears that change caused by a divorce can bring. See if any of these resonate with where you are today (again from chapter 10).

Fear of the unknown. As horrible as those last few weeks or months were prior to our divorces, at least we had some idea of what to expect. It's not knowing what's ahead as single-agains that can be maddening.

Fear of failure. Our marriages have failed. Will we fail as singles, too?

Fear of commitment. Our commitment to our marriages failed. What will happen to our commitments to emotional health? to other relationships? to God?

Fear of disapproval. Will others think less of us now that we are divorced?

Fear of success. If we're okay as single people, will God leave us single always?

4. Do you experience any of these fears? Write them down and explain how they show up in your life.

5. Have these fears kept you from accepting this new season of life?
   Explain.

Befriending Change

Befriending change does not mean you have to communicate that everything in life is now fine and dandy. Accepting change doesn't mean that you believe in divorce or think it's a wonderful change to be embraced and applauded. Befriending this change means that you accept it is happening, and you are going to take steps to move forward despite your fears or anxiety.

Try these practical tools summarized from chapter 10 to help you take your next steps.

Start with small, specific, limited goals. Maybe your ultimate goal is a new set of activities to take the place of some of the things you did as a married couple. The best way to approach that goal is to add a small thing to your daily routine. This might be the perfect time to take a class at the local community college or read that book you have always wanted to read. This is a great opportunity to join a health club or go on that diet or start writing that mystery novel you've had in the back of your mind.

Focus on proactive change instead of reactive change. Don't wait for further change to be forced upon you. Move forward.

Choose to stretch yourself. Try something you normally wouldn't do. Don't box yourself in with the thought, *Well, I've always done things this way, so...* Risk a little, and see what happens.

Spread out your sources of identity. Perhaps you always thought of yourself as so-and-so's wife or as so-and-so, the family guy. Maybe your entire identity was wrapped up in being married. You are more than a spouse. You are a worker, a friend, a child of God. Many things define you. Branch out and see if you might also be a fisherwoman or a woodworking guy or a sports person.

Take care of yourself. Sometimes it can be easy to focus on everyone but yourself. Your needs may fall by the wayside as you run from the emotions you are feeling. Stop. Be still. Rest. And take care of yourself.

6. As you read through the list, which item resonates with you? Explain.

7. What steps can you take to incorporate that tool into your life? Be specific.

GOD'S VIEW OF CHANGE

In chapter 10 of *New Life After Divorce,* Bill uses the Old Testament story of Joshua to remind us of three things we can cling to in the midst of change.

God's promise. God has promised that He is able to meet you in the middle of uncertainty. He is your refuge and strength. He has abundant and eternal life for you. Holding on to these truths will keep you steady in the midst of change.

God's power. God's power is in His Word, the Bible. His truth is our ultimate source of healing, encouragement, and energy. He gives us the power we need to make it day by day as we spend time reading, reflecting, and meditating on His Word.

God's presence. You don't ever have to feel alone. God is with you. Even though your former spouse left you, that's not the way God operates. He wants to embrace you and let you know that, together, the two of you can do anything. He knows you hurt. He knows you feel burned. He knows how reluctant you are to trust anyone again. He knows all about those feelings, and He is ready and able to comfort you.

> Have I not commanded you? Be strong and courageous!
> Do not tremble or be dismayed, for the LORD your God
> is with you wherever you go. (Joshua 1:9)

8. Are you able to take comfort from God's Word? Why or why not?

9. Which specific truth is most meaningful to you right now—God's promise, power, or presence? Explain why, and thank God for the reminder of His faithfulness.

NEW BEGINNINGS

As we encounter and work through the change that divorce has brought, new beginnings await. Sometimes, however, reaching that new beginning requires an extra dose of perseverance and strength. You may run into issues that seem insurmountable—loneliness, financial stress, parenting alone. In chapter 12 Bill calls this "hitting the wall." He talks about how runners have coined the phrase "hitting the wall" to describe the moment when you feel you can't take another step. Every muscle aches; every bone and joint rings out with pain. You want to quit. You want to stop. You want to give up. This is the very moment when we must persevere, because on the other side of that wall lies our second wind.

Any one of the emotions that accompany divorce can cause us to throw up our hands and quit.

> The wall in your life…could be dealing with *disappointment*, as you find yourself saying, "I didn't think it would turn out this way." Or perhaps it's *regret,* saying,

"I wish I had done things differently." Maybe your wall is *failure:* "I just blew it completely in a particular area of my life."

The wall in your life could be *frustration,* which says, "I feel so unsettled; I'm just churning inside." *Confusion* is another wall. "It should have worked. I can't understand why it didn't." Or, more seriously, perhaps *depression* is your wall. "I'm sad—all the time—about everything."

Maybe *lethargy* or *fatigue* has become your wall. "I've lost my energy for life." Or *isolation,* which says, "I've been burned once, so…I'm not going to expose myself to that kind of pain ever again.…" The wall in your life could be *fear* or *anxiety,* which says, "I'm scared!"

Or maybe the wall in your life is that you have *lost the ability to dream.* "Why should I dream? My dreams never come true!" Or life is *no fun.* "It's the same ol' boring routine." Worst of all, the wall in your life could be that you have *lost hope.* 📖

10. Which one of these walls has stopped your growth through this change? Or are there several? Jot them down here.

11. Have you been able to push through these things to find your second wind? If so, how? If not, read on.

How Do I Get a Second Wind?

Change has come. Maybe you've incorporated some positive strategies in your life, and now you've run into a wall of anger, depression, or frustration. Whatever the case may be, there's help and hope. Here are some tools you can use to break through these walls.

Be proactive. We have talked about the need to give yourself time and distance in order to allow God to heal your soul. How much time? It's a case-by-case call. But we can sometimes use that knowledge to justify standing still. We all have to reach the point where we pick ourselves up, dust ourselves off, and get back in the race.

Face your giants. Something (guilt, jealousy, lust) has come into your life and robbed you of your joy. But just as God equipped David to knock out the giant Goliath with five smooth stones, He can equip you to break through this wall. Call out to Him. Trust His strength. He is bigger.

Make the right choices. Sometimes it's tempting to detour down the wrong path because we've been hurt. We're trying to make it through this change, we've hit a wall, and now we feel justified to go racing into sin. Don't go there. Make the right choices no matter the circumstances. They will help you make it through this wall.

Take your stand. Once you make the decision to stand for what is right, temptation will come. Don't waver. Stand firm. God's second wind awaits. Don't jeopardize it by heading down the wrong road.

Learn the lessons in waiting. You've hit a wall. You find yourself stuck. God may have something for you in this very moment. If it's taking time to move through this issue, what can you learn from God in the meantime? What is He teaching you?

Appreciate God's good gifts. Sometimes when we're focused on one particular frustration, we forget to see what God is doing with the rest of our lives. We don't see that He's provided food on the table, a friend's smile, or a verse to remind us of His love. Keep your eyes open. God has something for you. And as you see it, you'll be better able to push through to your second wind.

Be available. Rather than giving up, put your life and future into the hand of God. Spend time with Him in prayer, in conversation, in worship. And as you submit this area of your life to Him, He will break through anything in your path and usher you into the place of new beginnings and second winds.

12. Of the previous tools, which one is most difficult for you right now? Explain.

13. What steps can you take to incorporate it in your life? Be specific.

As you consider walking through this change, pushing through the tough issues and encountering a second wind, you might feel overwhelmed by all the information. Take a moment to write a note from your heart to God. Ask Him to show you what you need to do next, and then trust Him to help you do it.

DISCUSSION QUESTIONS

If you are working with a group, answer the following questions in the group.

14. Do you feel as though you are moving through this change? Have you hit any walls? Explain.

15. What was especially meaningful to you in this last session? How has God met you?

16. How can the group pray specifically for you?

ALSO AVAILABLE FROM BILL BUTTERWORTH

WATERBROOK PRESS
www.waterbrookpress.com